Kaplan Publishing's learning materials are designed to help students succeed in their examinations. In certain circumstances, CIMA can make post-exam adjustment to a student's mark or grade to reflect adverse circumstances which may have disadvantaged a student's ability to take an exam or demonstrate their normal level of attainment (see CIMA's Special Consideration policy). However, it should be noted that students will not be eligible for special consideration by CIMA if preparation for or performance in a CIMA exam is affected by any failure by their tuition provider to prepare them properly for the exam for any reason including, but not limited to, staff shortages, building work or a lack of facilities etc.

Similarly, CIMA will not accept applications for consider

- failu
  sylla

- failu
  for in
  throu

- failure by the student to prepare adequately for the exam, or to use the correct pre-seen material

- errors in the Kaplan Official Study Text, including sample (practice) questions or any other Kaplan content or

- errors in any other study materials (from any other tuition provider or publisher).

## How to use Revision Cards

## The concept

- Revision Cards are a new and different way of learning, based upon research into learning styles and effective recall.

- The cards are in full colour and have text supported by a range of images, making them far more effective for visual learners and easier to remember.

- Unlike a bound text, Revision Cards can be rearranged and reorganised to appeal to kinaesthetic learners who prefer to learn by doing.

- Being small enough to carry around means that you can take them anywhere. This gives the opportunity to keep going over what you need to learn and so helps with recall.

- The content has been reduced down to the most important areas, making it far easier to digest and identify the relationships between key topics.

- Revision Cards, however you learn, whoever you are, wherever you are.........

### How to use them

Revision Cards are a pack of approximately 52 cards, slightly bigger than traditional playing cards but still very easy to carry and so convenient to use when travelling or moving around. They can be used during the tuition period or at revision.

They are broken up into 3 sections.

- An overview of the entire subject in a mind map form (orange).

- A mind map of each specific topic (blue).

- Content for each topic presented so that it is memorable (green).

Each one is a different colour, allowing you to sort them in many ways.

- Perhaps you want to get a more detailed feel for each topic, why not take all the green cards out of the pack and use those.

- You could create your own mind maps using the blue cards to explore how different topics fit together.

- And if there are some topics that you understand, take those out of the pack, leaving yourself only the ones you need to concentrate on.

There are just so many ways you can use them.

**Contents**

1. The roles of the finance function in organisations

2. The activities performed by finance professionals to fulfil the roles

3. The structure and shape of the finance function

4. What each level of the finance function does

5. Technology affecting business and finance

6. How the finance function uses digital technologies

7. Data and the finance function

8. Data to create and preserve value for organisations

9. How the finance function interacts with operations

10. How the finance function interacts with sales and marketing

11. How the finance function interacts with human resources

12. How the finance function interacts with IT

## Exam guidance
### Format of the exam

E1 is tested in two ways:

1. A 90 minute computerised objective test exam.
- 60 questions, equally weighted.
- Questions will be drawn from across individual subjects of the syllabus in line with syllabus weightings
- A range of question types will be used. The main types will be multiple choice, multiple response, hot spot, fill in the blank (number entry) and drag and drop.
2. In the 3 hour operational level computerised integrated case study.
- Set within a simulated business context.
- Contains four equally weighted sections.
- Tests a wide variety of skills and knowledge across each level.

### Core areas of the syllabus

| | | |
|---|---|---|
| A | Role of the finance function | 20% |
| B | Technology in a digital world | 20% |
| C | Data and information in a digital world | 20% |
| D | Shape and structure of the finance function | 20% |
| E | Finance interacting with the organisation | 20% |

Quality and accuracy are of the utmost importance to us so if you spot an error in any of our products, please send an email to mykaplanreporting@kaplan.com with full details, or follow the link to the feedback form in MyKaplan.

Our Quality Co-ordinator will work with our technical team to verify the error and take action to ensure it is corrected in future editions.

RevisionCards

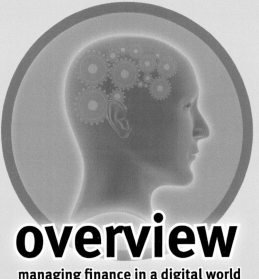

# overview

### managing finance in a digital world

The roles of the finance function in organisations

The activities performed by finance professionals to fulfil the roles

**Role of the finance function**

The finance function's relationship to operations

How the finance function uses digital technologies

The finance function's relationship to sales and marketing

Technology affecting business and finance

**Finance interacting with the organisation**

**Technology in a digital world**

**Managing finance in a digital world**

The finance function's relationship to human resources

The finance function's relationship to IT

**Data and information in a digital world**

Data and the finance function

**Shape and structure of the finance function**

Data to create and preserve value for the organisation

What each level of the finance function does

The structure and shape of the finance function

# the roles of the finance function in organisations

managing finance in a digital world

RevisionCards

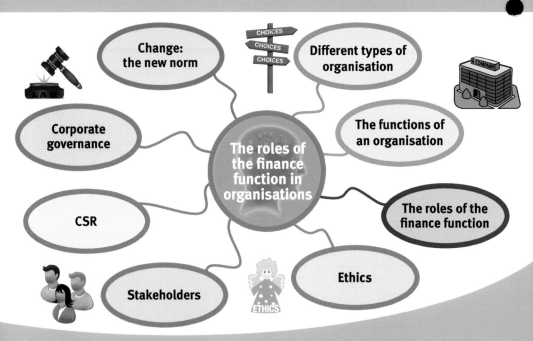

## Change: the new norm

> Change is the new norm in many organisations due to seismic shifts in the level of **competition,** customers' expectations, the global political outlook and fast paced **technological change**.

- These changes present both **risks** and **opportunities**.
- These changes will impact the **organisation** and the **finance function** within it.

## Different types of organisation

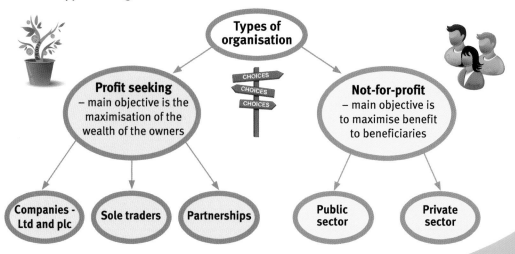

## The roles of the finance function

Finance is one of the functions of an organisation. Others include operations, sales and marketing, human resources and IT.

**1. ENABLES** organisations to create and preserve value

- Planning
- Forecasting
- Resource allocation

**2. SHAPES HOW** organisations create and preserve value

- Performance management
- Control

**3. NARRATES HOW** organisations create and preserve value

- Financial (corporate) reporting

Value is the achievement of the specified objective(s) most economically and at the required standard of quality and reliability. The three roles create value in the short-term and preserve value for the longer-term.

## Ethics and corporate social responsibility (CSR)

**Ethics** is the system of moral principles that examines the concept of right and wrong. **Business ethics** is the application of ethical values to business behavior.

CIMA's ethical principles:

1. Integrity
2. Objectivity
3. Professional competence and due care
4. Confidentiality
5. Professional behaviour

**Corporate social responsibility (CSR)**

CSR means that the company is **sensitive to the needs of all stakeholders and not just shareholders.**

## Stakeholders

- A stakeholder is a group or individual, who has an **interest** in what the organisation does or an **expectation** of the organisation.
- There are three types; **internal, connected** and **external.**

If an organisation is having difficulty deciding who the dominant stakeholder is, they can use Mendelow's power-interest matrix.

| | | |
|---|---|---|
| **High** | | |
| **Power** | **Keep satisfied** | **Key players** |
| **Low** | **Minimal effort** | **Keep informed** |
| | Low    **Interest**    High | |

## Corporate governance

- **Corporate governance** is the set of processes and policies by which a company is directed, administered and controlled.
- The need arises due to the **seperation of ownership and control** which results in a potential **agency problem.**

The **UK Corporate Governance Code** sets out guidelines on the:

- Use of the AGM
- Board
- Chairman and CEO
- Non-executive directors (NEDs)
- Nomination committee
- Remuneration committee
- Audit committee

# the activities performed by finance professionals to fulfil the roles

managing finance in a digital world

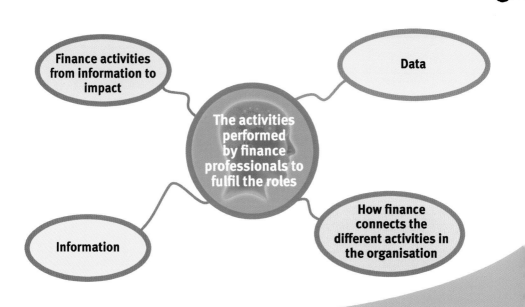

## Finance activities from information to impact

The basic activities that finance professionals perform can be summarised using the **'information to impact' framework**. The framework has **four sequential stages** to value creation and preservation and there are **five linking activities (the 5 A's)**.

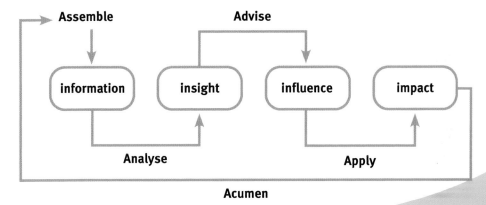

The **information to impact framework can be expanded** as follows:

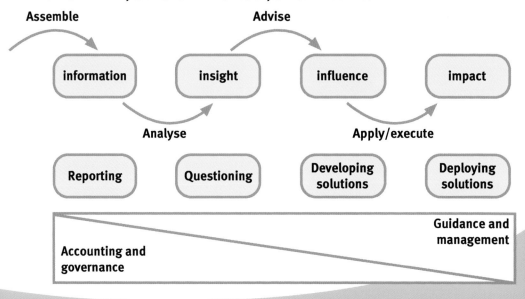

## Data

> **Data** is defined as facts or figures in a raw, unprocessed form.

**External sources** include:

- suppliers
- customers
- newspapers, journals, the internet
- the government

These sources will have their **limitations.**

**Internal sources** include:

- accounting records
- payroll data
- production data
- sales and marketing data

## Information

> **Information** is data that has been processed in such a way that it has meaning to the person who receives it.
>
> Finance professionals **'assemble'** and then **'analyse'** it for insights.
>
> **Technology** will play a key role in capturing information.

Qualities of **Good information ('accurate')**:

- **A**ccurate
- **C**omplete
- **C**ost < benefit
- **U**nderstandable
- **R**elevant
- **A**daptable/**A**ccessible
- **T**imely
- **E**asy to use

## Types of information

**1. Financial** – this will be **quantitative** (numerical in nature)

Finance may make **mistakes when analysing quantitative information** for insights:
- Analysis based on inappropriately presented information
- Failure to evaluate figures using a suitable comparator
- Data sampling inappropriate resulting in information which is not 'good'.

**2. Non-Financial** – this will be **quantitative** or **qualitative** (non-numerical in nature)

- Main limitation of **qualitative information** is that judgement is needed due to its subjective nature
- Overcome by looking at trends or transforming into quantitative information.

## How finance connects the different activities in the organisation

**1** It provides information and insight to other functions **enabling** them to create and preserve value.

**2** It works with other functions to **shape how** the function creates and preserves value.

**3** It works with other functions to achieve the desired organisational impact for the function, **narrating how** the finance creates and preserves value.

# the structure and shape of the finance function

**managing finance in a digital world**

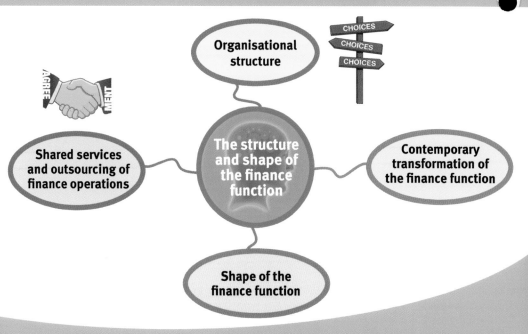

## Organisational structure

**Organisational structure** is formed by the grouping of people into departments or sections and the allocation of responsibility and authority.

**Mintzberg** suggested that an organisation can be split into **six building blocks** and that effective **co-ordination** will be needed.

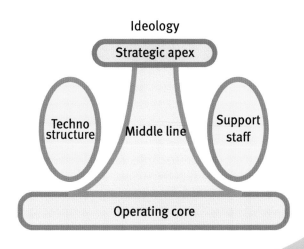

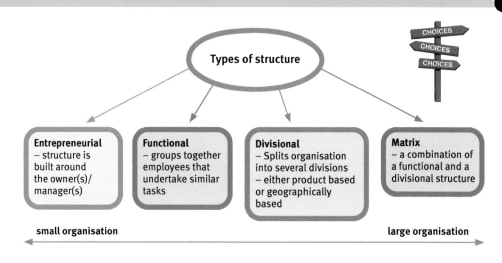

There are **advantages** and **disadvantages** associated with each structure.

**Centralisation and decentralisation**
refers to the level at which decisions are made

In a **centralised** structure, the upper levels of the organisation's hierarchy retain the authority to make decisions

In a **decentralised** structure, the authority to make decisions is passed down to units and people at lower levels

There are **advantages** and **disadvantages** associated with each of these.

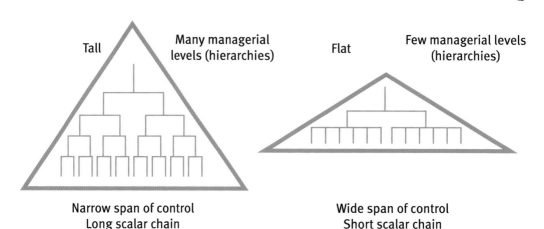

## Contemporary transformation of the finance function

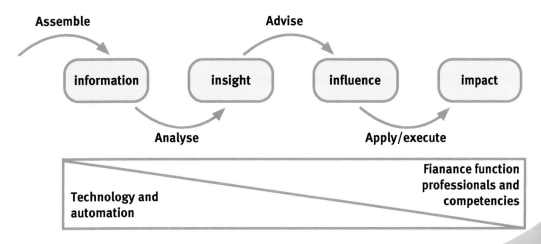

**Historically,** the mandate of the finance function was to focus on **organisational efficiencies** and to **reduce operational costs**.

**Technology** now allows machines to monitor operational costs and patterns of organisational efficiency.

The finance function should view this as an **oppotunity** and **not a threat.**

It can **refocus its energy on revenue and value creation, working with others and across the organisation** to drive business transformation and to create shareholder value.

## Shape of the finance function

The **shape is evolving** as a result of advances in **technology,** the **changing mandate** of the finance function and the **changing capabilities** of the finance function.

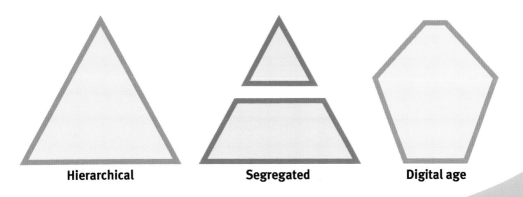

| Hierarchical | Segregated | Digital age |

The **traditional hierarchical triangle** can be understood in the context of the three roles of **enabling, shaping how** and **narrating how** the organisation creates and preserves value.

A narrower group of senior finance staff concentrate on the **'narrating how'** role of financial (corporate) reporting.

A narrower set of management level finance workers carry out the **'shaping how'** roles of performance management and control.

A broad base of finance workers carry out the operational **'enabling'** roles of planning, forecasting and resource allocation.

- Over the last 20 years the **shape has migrated from a traditional hierarchical shape to a segregated triangle.**

- The bottom section of the segregated triangle represents the finance function activity carried out by a **shared service centre (SSC);** the centralisation of routine processing into one place.

**Establishment of SSC driven by two main factors**

**Globalisation**
- Many organisations grew in size with operations and processing centres in several countries.
- A SSC enabled the consolidation of these activities to one site.

**Advances in technology**
- Enabling automation of many of the lower level tasks carried out by the finance function.

The tradition hierarchical triangle is evolving into a **diamond shape** as follows:

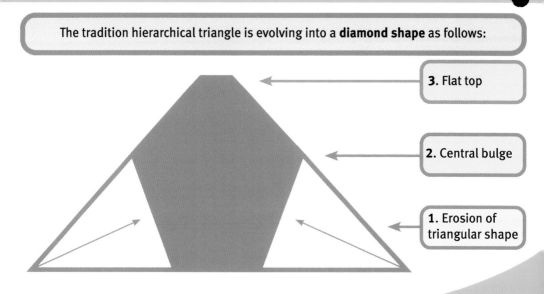

**3.** Flat top

**2.** Central bulge

**1.** Erosion of triangular shape

**1** Technology has **eroded the traditional triangular shape** – lower level assembly and processing tasks are now carried out by technology and not finance.

**2** The **central bulge** is due to many higher – value activities now being carried out by centres of excellence (or shared service centres).

**3** The **flat top** shows a move to a collaborative finance leadership approach – the CFO works with and alongside the CEO.

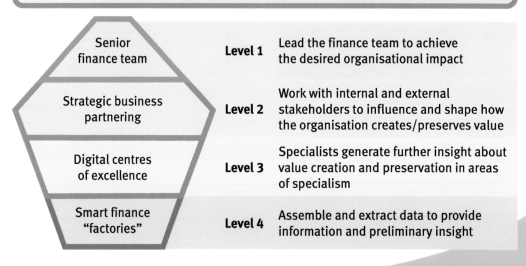

The diamond shape can be split into four levels.

| | | |
|---|---|---|
| Senior finance team | **Level 1** | Lead the finance team to achieve the desired organisational impact |
| Strategic business partnering | **Level 2** | Work with internal and external stakeholders to influence and shape how the organisation creates/preserves value |
| Digital centres of excellence | **Level 3** | Specialists generate further insight about value creation and preservation in areas of specialism |
| Smart finance "factories" | **Level 4** | Assemble and extract data to provide information and preliminary insight |

## Shared services and outsourcing of finance operations

- **Outsourcing** means contracting out aspects of the work of the organisation previously done in-house, to specialist providers.

- **Outsourcing of the finance function's activities** (particularly 'assembly' and 'analysis' tasks) have become increasingly common.

| Advantages | Disadvantages |
| --- | --- |
| <ul><li>Cost reduction</li><li>Shift resources from operations to innovation</li><li>Retained finance function can concentrate on role as business partners</li><li>Access to superior capabilities and resources</li></ul> | <ul><li>Loss of control</li><li>Time and cost to manage the service</li><li>Disruption and resistance to change</li><li>Risk of data theft/breaches</li><li>Erosion of internal knowledge and skills</li></ul> |

- **A shared service centre** may be established for a particular activity of the organisation. The term describes a situation whereby, a usually large, multinational organisation with processing centres in all or several of the countries in which it operates chooses to consolidate these activities at one site, or shared service centre. This is sometimes referred to as **'internal outsourcing'**.

- As the shape of the finance function evolves there is an opportunity for shared service centres to offer **not only the level 4 activities but also the level 3 and level 2 activities (diamond shape)**.

# what each level of the finance function does

**managing finance in a digital world**

## Finance operations (level 4)

| | |
|---|---|
| **Financial (corporate) reporting** | Concerned with the production of financial information for external users in accordance with relevant accounting standards and legislation. |
| **Management accounting** | The provision of information to help managers and other internal users in their decision making, performance measurement, planning and controlling activities. |
| **Treasury management** | The management of the funds of the business (cash and working capital) plus long-term investments, debt and equity. |
| **Internal audit** | Independently evaluates risk management processes and systems of control to make recommendations for the achievement of organisation's objectives. |

## Specialist areas (level 3)

The specialists are experts who provide insight derived from the information handed to them a level 4.

| FP&A | • Perform budgeting, forecasting, data analysis and support board decisions<br>• Help continued profitability and growth |
|---|---|
| Taxation | • Tax compliance – follow laws and regulations to minimise risk<br>• Tax planning – to legally minimise tax paid and create value |
| Project appraisal | • Evalutes the decisions and potential outcomes of a project<br>• Uses methods such as payback, NPV and IRR |
| Project management | • Integrates all aspects of a project ensuring proper knowledge and resources<br>• Ensures expected outcome is produced in a timely, cost effective manner |

## Strategic partnering for value (level 2)

The insights that level 3 provide are passed on to finance professionals working as strategic partners.

### Communicating insight to influence users

These strategic partners will interpret and use financial statements and other data to:

- communicate this insight
- in an appropriate format
- and required frequency
- to internal and external stakeholders

to influence users of this information in their decision making and implementation of control activities.

### Business partnering

- Influences the organisation's activities to achieve the desired impact.
- Successful finance business partners are seen as leaders who can influence decision making to maximise value.
- Business partnering may be provided by finance function employees working alongside departmental managers, a multi-disciplinary team in a centre of excellence or a mix of both.

## Strategic leadership of the finance team (level 1)

The head of the finance function is the chief financial officer (**CFO**) and it is their responsibility to lead the finance team to achieve the desired organisational **impact**.

- Lead key initiatives that support organisational goals
- Execute and fund strategies set by the CEO
- Liaise effectively with internal and external stakeholders

CFOs increasingly work alongside the CEO as **co-pilot** in the success of the business.

## The impact of technology on the activities of finance professionals

Organisations are using technology to automate management information processes and to provide reporting to the rest of the business on a self-serve basis.

- This has resulted in a narrowing of the level 4 activities.
- At the same time it has increased the need for skills and talent at levels 3 and 2.

A McKinsey report studied which functions could be automated by advancing technology.

Leading the finance team

Managing others (9%)

Stakeholder interactions (20%)

Partnering for value to influence and shape how the organisation creates and preserves value

Applying expertise (18%)

Specialists generating further insights in their areas of specialism

Data processing (69%)

Assembling and extracting data and providing limited insight

Data collection (64%)

# technology affecting business and finance

## managing finance in a digital world

RevisionCards

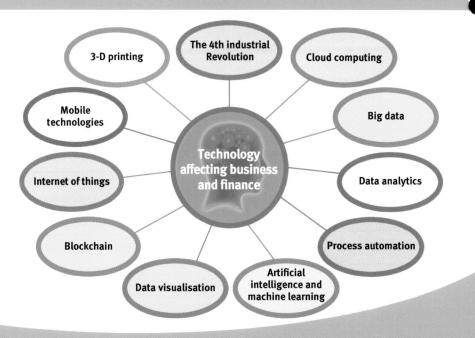

## The 4th Industrial Revolution

An **industrial revolution** is a **rapid** and major change in an economy, driven by a shift in the methods and types of work undertaken.

The pace of technological change and innovation that is influencing the way we trade, work, travel, socialise and live our everyday lives continues to accelerate.

Analysts and experts predict the rate of this change will increase, driving another fundamental shift in society and the global economy and hence it has been termed the **4th Industrial Revolution**.

There are a number of key technologies driving the digital world.

## Cloud computing

Cloud computing is defined as **the delivery of on-demand computing resources**. Users log into an account in order to access, manage and process files and software via remote servers hosted on the internet. The cloud setup can be **public** or **private**.

### Advantages

- Flexibility and scalability
- Cost efficient
- Security
- Flexible working
- Environment

### Disadvantages

- Organisational change
- Contract management
- Security, privacy and reliance
- Contract management

## Big data

Big data describes data sets (structured and unstructured) so large and varied they are beyond the capability of traditional data-processing.

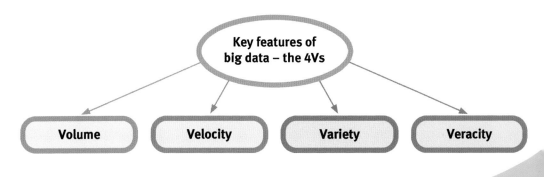

## Data analytics

Data analytics is the process of collecting, organising and analysing large sets of data (big data) to discover patterns and other information which the organisation can use to inform future decisions.

### Benefits (McKinsey):

- Fresh insight and understanding

- Performance improvement

- Improved segmentation and customisation

- Better decision making

- Innovation

- Risk management

## Process automation

**The technology enabled automation of complex business processes**. This can be entire processes or elements therein aimed at improving consistency, quality, speed, whilst delivering cost savings.

Some of the technological developments described in this chapter enable advanced process automation, now capable of making decisions using reasoning, language and learned behaviour.

**Professions most at risk** from automation include data entry, tax preparation, insurance underwriters, mathematical technicians, telemarketers and accounts clerks.

**Professions least at risk** from automation include social workers, healthcare assistants, audiologists, occupational therapists, recreational therapists and mental health professionals.

## Artificial intelligence and machine learning

**Artificial intelligence (AI)** is an area of computer science that emphasises the creation of intelligent machines that work and react like human beings.

**Machine learning** is a subset of AI, in which AI computer code is built to effectively mimic how the human brain works.

Activities and skills AI can master include:

**Voice recognition**  **Planning**  **Learning**  **Problem solving**

## Data visualisation

Allows large volumes of complex data to be displayed in a visually appealing and accessible way that facilitates the understanding and use of the underlying data.

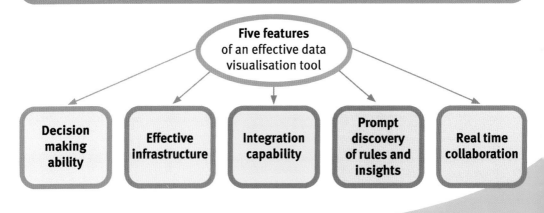

**Five features** of an effective data visualisation tool

- Decision making ability
- Effective infrastructure
- Integration capability
- Prompt discovery of rules and insights
- Real time collaboration

## Blockchain

A blockchain is a decentralised, distributed and public ledger that is used to record transaction across many computers.

**Benefits:**

- Security
- Decentralised
- Transparency
- Traceability and completeness
- Reduced fraud risk

## Internet of things

Describes the network of smart devices with inbuilt software and connectivity to the internet allowing them to constantly monitor and exchange data.

Common devices connected as part of the internet of things:

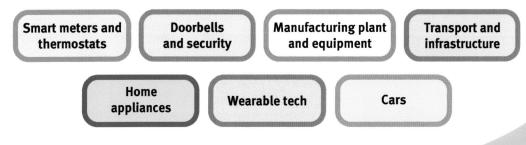

## Mobile technologies

**Code division multiple access (CDMA)** is the technology that underpins mobile technology.

- The rapid development in mobile technology has emerged at the same time as huge advances in internet technology and connectivity.

- Together these technologies support or fuel many of the technologies discussed in this chapter. They are fuelling big changes in consumer activity.

## 3-D printing

3-D printing is part of a process known as additive manufacturing where the object is created layer by layer. It allows complex parts and components to be produced cheaper, faster and in an entirely customisable fashion.

**Benefits:**

- Speed
- Cost effectiveness
- Customisation
- Less waste
- Confidentiality

# how the finance function uses digital technologies

## managing finance in a digital world

How the finance function uses digital technologies

Digital mindsets

How the finance function uses digital technologies

Ethical, legal and social considerations of technology

## New technologies and finance

The technologies introduced in the previous chapter will impact the finance function.

**Core modernisation tools** – update existing systems and improve capability. Include cloud technology and data visualisation.

**Exponentials** – deliver new capabilities and push the finance function forward. Include blockchain and advanced analytics.

**Cloud computing** has changed the structure and working of the finance function:

| | |
|---|---|
| **Collaboration** | Multiple collaborators can update documents in real time. |
| **Flexible working** | Enabled by access to your desktop from anywhere with an internet connection. |
| **Increased security** | Service providers understand that data security (especially financial data) is critical to their success. |
| **Up to date** | Continually up to date software helps ensure compliance with regulations such as GDPR. |
| **Easier integration** | Cloud based accounting software can easily integrate with other cloud based software and is designed for scalability. |

**Big data and data analytics** – accountants will increasingly occupy a business partnering role acting as the interface between data scientists and the business by making the data relevant and commercial.

Big data/data analytics and elements of the finance function:

| | |
|---|---|
| **Management accounting** | Will result in more efficient and insightful budgeting and control. |
| **Financial accounting** | Will improve the quality, relevance and transparency of information. |
| **Reporting** | Will assist with the creation and improvement of accounting standards. |
| **Internal audit** | Will enable internal audit to better identify anomalies, fraud and risk, tailoring their approach to target more business critical areas. |

Advantages and disadvantages of process automation technology within the finance function include:

| Advantages | Disadvantages |
|---|---|
| • Cost savings | • Uncertainty |
| • Focus on value adding activities | • Relationship management |
| • Improved accuracy | • Competence |
| • Positive return | • Training |
| • Adaptability | • Change management |

Examples of **AI** impacting the finance function:

**1** Coding of accounting entries, improved accuracy of rules-based approaches, enabling **greater automation of processes**.

**2** Sophisticated, machine learning models can understand 'normal' activities to **better identify fraudulent activities**.

**3** Using machine learning based **predictive models** to forecast revenues.

**4** Recommend supplier specific discounts to **optimise cash at hand**.

**5** Extraction of **insights** from real-time data without information overload.

**Data visualisation and the finance function** – the provision of information to help support the efficient and effective running of all functions within a business overall is the fundamental purpose of the finance function.

**Blockchain technology** such as cryptocurrencies, present both opportunities and challenges to the finance function. Examples of how blockchain can enhance the accounting profession include:

- Improving the cash position by better managing resources

- Reducing the cost of maintaining and reconciling ledgers

- Providing certainty over ownership/history of assets

- Help accountants gain clarity over available resources

- Free up resources to concentrate on value adding activities rather than record keeping.

## Digital mindsets

A **digital mindset** is the concept of seeing beyond the individual elements of digital technology, to understand the deeper all-pervading ways in which digital technology will ultimately transform every aspect of society and therefore impact the organisation.

**Dimensions include:**

- Provide vision yet empower others

- Give up control yet architect the choices

- Sustain yet disrupt

- Rely on data yet trust your intuition

- Be sceptical yet open minded.

A fundamental element of a digital mindset is being **change adept**, that is being capable of and ready for change. One part of this will be having finance professionals with a **growth mindset**, meaning:

- an appetite to learn and develop

- feedback openly given and positively received

- change embraced and seen as an opportunity.

## Ethics of technology usage

Data is a central aspect of many of the technological developments discussed. **General Data Protection Regulation (GDPR)** outlines the following principles about data and data usage:

- Used fairly, lawfully and transparently

- Used for specified, explicit purposes

- Used in a way that is adequate, relevant and limited to only what is necessary

- Accurate and, where required, kept up to date

- Kept no longer than is necessary

- Handled to ensure appropriate security.

**Corporate digital responsibility (CDR)** goes beyond compliance with statutory regulations and involves a commitment to protecting both customers and employees and ensuring that new technologies and data are used both productively and wisely.

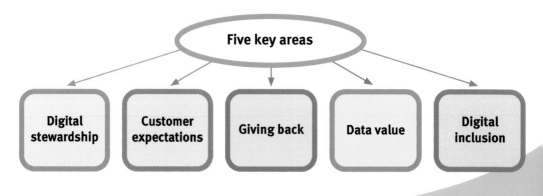

Five key areas

| Digital stewardship | Customer expectations | Giving back | Data value | Digital inclusion |

# data and the finance function

## managing finance in a digital world

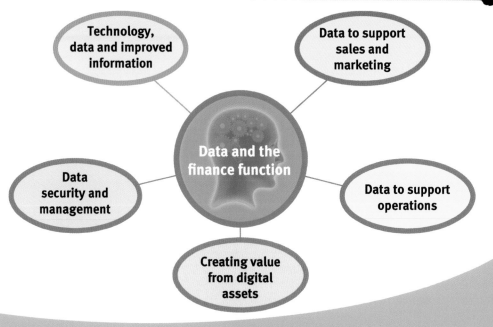

**Technology, data and improved information**

- The technological developments already discussed are providing and utilising data on a new level, which if harnessed correctly can provide high value information, facilitating enhanced decision making at all levels (strategic, tactical and operational) of an organisation.

- In this chapter we will look more closely at the growing importance of data and how it is being used by the finance function to assemble information, analyse it for insight, advise to influence and apply for impact.

- We will also look at how data is used by businesses across their various functions.

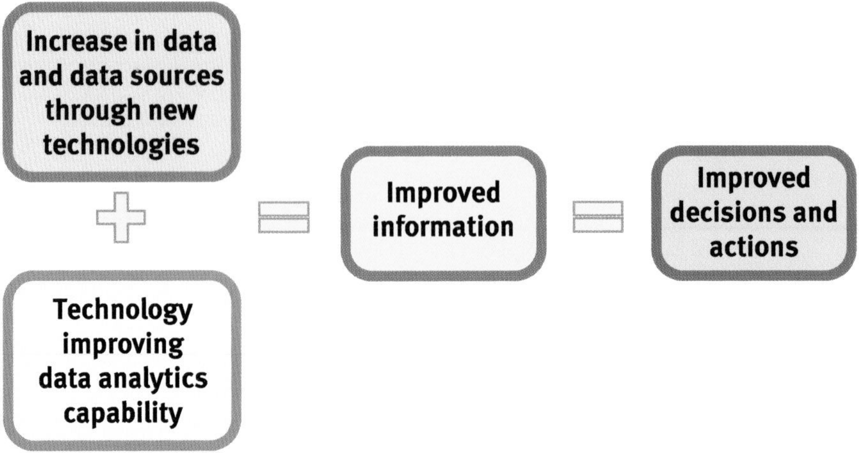
Increase in data and data sources through new technologies
+
Technology improving data analytics capability
=
Improved information
=
Improved decisions and actions

## Data to support sales and marketing

The data available is providing real, fact based insight into customers and competitors actions resulting in improved sales and marketing decisions:

| | | |
|---|---|---|
| **Optimum product development and mix** | **Identification and refinement of segments** | **Which promotions work best and when** |
| **Improved pricing decisions** | **Improved targeting** | **Optimum CRM to fulfil specific needs** |

## Data to support operations

Capturing and analysing new sources of operational data is driving change and improvements in operations leading to benefits such as:

- Costs savings through efficiency gains
- Service improvements
- Supply chain integration
- Customised products
- Preventative maintenance
- Forecasting facilitating efficient operations
- Early warning of potential problems

## Creating value from digital assets

**Digital assets** are held by a business in a digital form and do not have physical substance. Typically includes images, animations, audio, video and PDF files.

A **digital asset management system (DAM)** is designed to coordinate the digital assets of the business, ensuring they are held centrally in an accessible, secure and logically designed repository. Features of DAM systems include:

- Specialised, typically cloud based, database

- Single, central location

- Security and access levels built in

- Clear categorisation and search capability using metadata

**Data protection** can be defined as the process of safeguarding important information from corruption, compromise or loss. Businesses as a minimum must comply with GDPR.

The following are some of the features of modern organisations and their approach to sound **data management:**

- Chief Data Officer (CDO) role

- Deliberate and integrated data strategy

- Culture promotes the significance of data

- Data security training

# data to create and preserve value for organisations

## managing finance in a digital world

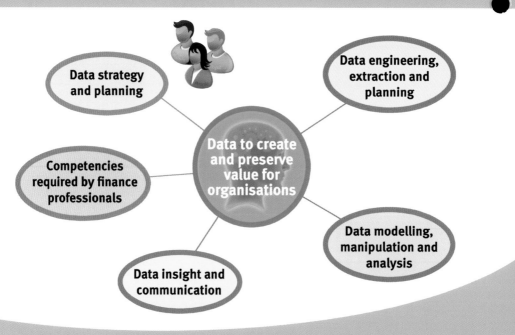

## Competencies required by finance professionals

The competencies can be grouped into **five types** and will be underpinned by **ethics, integrity and professionalism**.

| | |
|---|---|
| **Technical skills** | Application of accounting and finance skills |
| **Business skills** | Knowledge of data sources, analytical skills and judgement |
| **People skills** | Building empathy and interactions with stakeholders |
| **Leadership skills** | Team building, coaching and mentoring, driving performance and change management and the ability to motivate and inspire |
| **Digital skills** | For example, understanding information and data, data strategy and planning, data analytics and data visualisation. Both a standalone skill and permeates the other four skill areas. |

## Data strategy and planning

| Stakeholder | Data requirements |
|---|---|
| **Sales department** | Live data on competitors pricing and market trends. Metrics on key customer feedback. |
| **Production department** | Collection and recording of cost data. Live systems automatically reorder stock. |
| **HR department** | Data system to incorporate appraisal system, productivity analysis and data on internal progressions and training days. |
| **Shareholders** | A move to integrated reporting could see a shift in data needs and reporting. |
| **Employees** | In a unique position to flag inefficiencies in the system and suggest improvements. |
| **Managers and directors** | Data visualisations to summarise key metrics. |

## Data engineering, extraction and mining

**Extraction, transformation and loading (ETL)** are the three stages in transferring data. They are combined into a single tool to automatically bring data from various sources into a destination system.

**Business intelligence (BI)** is the technology driven processes of analysing business data to generate insightful and actionable information with a view to improving the operations or products of a business.

**ETL is a component of a wider BI process.** ETL provides the required data, BI accesses and analyses this data further for information and insight. Data visualisation is then used by BI to present findings to the wider business.

## Data modelling, manipulation and analysis

A **data model** considers the data of an organisation in a systematic way that allows it to be stored and retrieved in an efficient and effective manner. There are **three levels** of a data modeling process:

- **Conceptual**

- **Logical**

- **Physical**

**Data manipulation** is the process of changing data to make it easier to read. It involves adding, deleting, querying and modifying data in a data-store using a **data manipulation language (DML).**

## Data insight and communication

**Data strategy** is a coherent approach for organising, governing, analysing and deploying an organisation's information assets.

A business will need to cope with the attributes of big data (the 4V's) and the data strategy should consider the following:

| Volume | The capability to handle the sheer quantity of data |
| Velocity | How to process the millions of data points generated every minute |
| Variety | Internal, external, structured and unstructured |
| Veracity | System data must be validated |

**Data visualisations and the finance function** – in order to produce an effective data visualisation the following three questions should be considered:

1. Who are the audience?

2. How do they want the data?

3. What outcome do we want?

**Business focused data**

**Data scientists** are individuals with the ability to extract meaning from and interpret data, which requires both tools and methods from statistics and machine learning.

The **finance function acts as an interface** between these specialists and the other business functions.

# how the finance function interacts with operations

managing finance in a digital world

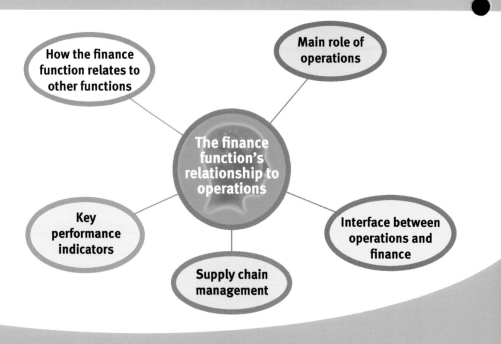

## How the finance function relates to other functions

**1** Assembles and extracts data to provide **information** to the other function and insight about value creation/preservation.

**2** Works with the other function and other stakeholders to **influence** and shape how this function creates and preserves value.

**3** The CFO will work with the head of each function to achieve the desired organisational **impact** for this function.

## Main role of operations

**Operations** are those activities concerned with the acquisition of raw materials, their conversion into finished products and the supply of the finished product to the customer.

| | | | |
|---|---|---|---|
| All operations consist of a collection of **processes** – these transform the inputs to outputs | **Processes are characterised by the 4 V's** – volume, variety, variation and visibility | **Process design** seeks to understand processes and design them to be as efficient and effective as possible | A **process map** provides a visual representation of the steps and decisions by which a product or transaction is processed |

The design of processes will go hand in hand with the design of new products/ services. The **stages in product/service development** are:

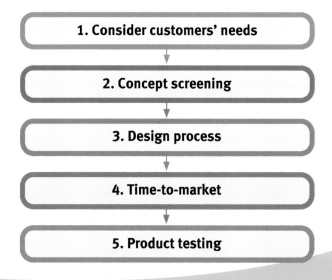

1. Consider customers' needs

2. Concept screening

3. Design process

4. Time-to-market

5. Product testing

**Porter's value chain** considers the **activities** (many of which relate to the operations function) that add value and drive costs and therefore the organisation should focus on improving.

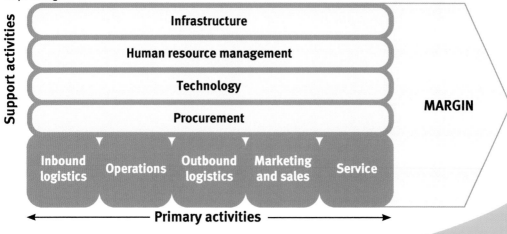

## Interface between operations and finance

| | |
|---|---|
| **Purchasing** | Will work with the finance function, for example, to seek advice on the best price to pay suppliers. |
| **Production** | Will work with the finance function, for example, to establish the optimum balance between cost and quality. |
| **Service provision** | Will work with the finance function, for example, to establish charge-out rates. |

## Supply chain management

A **supply chain** consists of a network of organisations. Together they provide and process the necessary raw materials firstly into work in progress and then into finished goods for sale and distribution to the end customer.

**Supply chain management (SCM)** involves the co-ordination of activities from the supplier(s) of raw materials at one end of the supply chain to the customer at the other end.

In this section we will understand:

- how the relationships within the supply chain can be managed and
- the interface between SCM and the finance function.

**Cousin's strategic supply wheel** depicts the corporate supply strategy at the hub of the wheel and underlines the need for an integrated approach to supply strategy involving a balancing of all spokes of the wheel.

**Relationships with suppliers** are an important aspect of the wheel:
- Past approach – competitive (contractual) relationship.
- Modern approach – collaborative (relational) approach.

**Systems available to ensure materials are ready when needed**

**Material requirement planning (MRP)** – a computerised system for planning requirements for raw material, work-in-progress and finished items.

**Manufacturing resource planning (II)** – an extension of MRP and includes, for example, production planning, demand forecasting and productivity tracking.

**Enterprise resource planning (ERP)** – the next evolution of MRP, integrating information from operations with that from other functions into a single system.

**Quality** is one of the key ways an organisation can differentiate its product or service.

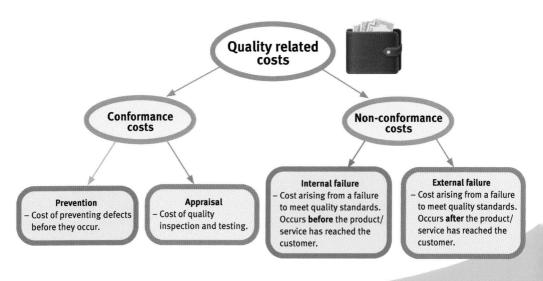

The following **techniques** can be used to **improve SCM**:

| Technique | Definition |
| --- | --- |
| **Statistical process control** | A method for measuring and controlling quality during a process. |
| **Total quality management (TQM)** | The continuous improvement in quality, productivity and effectiveness. |
| **Kaizen** | Continuous improvement in performance via small, incremental steps. |
| **Six Sigma** | Aims to achieve a reduction in the number of faults that go beyond an accepted tolerance level (3.4 defects in every one million). |
| **Lean thinking** | Aims to systematically eliminate waste through the identification and elimination of all non-value adding activities. |
| **Just-in-time (JIT)** | Procures inventory and produces products as they are required by the customer for use rather than for inventory. |
| **Reverse logistics** | The return of unwanted or surplus goods back to the organisation for reuse, recycling or disposal. |

It is important to understand the **interface between SCM and finance**:

- A **collaborative relationship** between the CFO and the leader of the supply chain is advantageous for organisational growth and competitive advantage.

- The finance function has a unique end to end view of the organisation and is considered a trusted advisor. As a result there are a number of **opportunities for finance to enhance performance through business partnering** with the supply chain.

- **Examples** include the establishment of appropriate KPIs or helping with the financial side of supplier relationships.

- **Technology** has been an important enabler in business partnering.

## Key performance indicators

**Critical success factors (CSFs)** are the vital areas 'where things must go right' for the business in order for them to achieve their strategic objectives.

**Key performance indicators (KPIs)** are the measures that indicate whether or not the CSFs are being achieved. Characteristics of good KPIs include:

- Cascade from strategy to tactics to operational level

- Cover all perspectives of operations

- Should be SMART

- Aligned to employees' reward system

- Extended to supply chain partners

**Examples of KPIs** for operations include:

- Supply chain costs per unit sold

- Time taken to deliver a customer order

- Percentage on-time delivery to a customer

- Percentage of customer orders fulfilled

- Percentage defect rates (suppliers and customers orders)

- Percentage wastage rate

| Finance function activity | How the finance function helps manage operations through the use of KPIs |
|---|---|
| Assembling information | • Works with operations to set appropriate KPIs.<br>• **Assembles** data and processes into useful KPI information.<br>• **Reports** information to those people who need it. |
| Analysing for insights | • Analyses KPI information to draw out patterns and relevant **insights** for those who use the information.<br>• The **questioning** may require the individual KPIs to be broken down. |
| Advising to influence | • Communicates insights and contributes an objective and responsible perspective to help develop **solutions** for problems identified.<br>• This will **influence** decision makers in the operations function. |
| Applying for impact **(execute)** | • Applies information to harness value for the operations function through its **impact**.<br>• **Solutions deployed** such as changes to future operational strategy and KPIs. |

# how the finance function interacts with sales and marketing

managing finance in a digital world

## Introduction to sales and marketing

> Marketing is defined by the Chartered Institute of Marketing as 'the management process that identifies, anticipates and supplies **customer needs** efficiently and profitably'.

**The market planning process:**

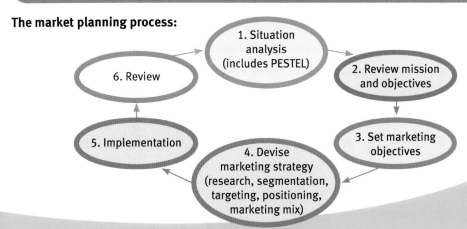

1. Situation analysis (includes PESTEL)

2. Review mission and objectives

3. Set marketing objectives

4. Devise marketing strategy (research, segmentation, targeting, positioning, marketing mix)

5. Implementation

6. Review

**Understanding the marketing mix** – the traditional marketing mix (4 P's)

| **P**roduct | Features, durability, design, branding, packaging, range, after-sales service, warranties, guarantees |
|---|---|
| **P**lace | Sell directly to consumer or indirectly using intermediaries such as wholesalers and retailers |
| **P**romotion | Advertising, personal selling, public relations, sales promotion, sponsorship, direct marketing and newer techniques (see over) |
| **P**rice | Price level (consider 4 C's), pricing strategies (see over), discounts, credit policy, payment terms |

There are three additional P's for the service industry –
**P**eople, **P**rocesses and **P**hysical evidence

| Pricing strategy | Explanation |
|---|---|
| **Cost-plus pricing** | Price based on cost plus % profit |
| **Penetration pricing** | Low price is set initially |
| **Skim pricing** | High price is set initially |
| **Perceived quality** | High price to reinforce high quality image |
| **Price discrimination** | Charge different prices for the same product in different segments |
| **Going rate pricing** | Price matches that of competitors |
| **Dynamic pricing** | Price altered in line with demand |
| **Loss leaders** | Product sold at a loss with the expectation other products will be bought |
| **Captive product** | For products bought together – the first is cheap, the second expensive |

| Newer form of promotion | Explanation |
|---|---|
| **Viral** | Encourages the individual to pass on the marketing message, creating exponential growth |
| **Guerrilla** | Well thought out, highly focused and often unconventional attacks on key targets |
| **Experiential** | An interactive, multi-sensory marketing experience |
| **Digital** | Uses electronic media such as email or the organisation's website |
| **Search engine marketing** | A form of digital marketing that aims to increase visibility in search engine results |
| **Social media marketing** | A form of digital marketing that aims to gain attention or traffic through social media sites |
| **Postmodern marketing** | A philosophical approach aiming to give the individual a customised experience |

## The main techniques of marketing

**Market research** is the systematic gathering, recording and analysing of quantitative and qualitative information about issues relating to the marketing of goods and services. These issues will all relate to what customers or potential customers want, need or care about. Data gathering techniques include:

- primary (field) research and
- secondary (desk) research.

**Market segmentation** is the sub-dividing of the market into homogenous groups to whom a separate marketing mix can be focused. Bases for segmentation include:

- demographic
- socio-economic
- psychological.

**Targeting** is the process of selecting the most lucrative market segment(s) for marketing the product. Choices include:

- concentrated (or niche/target) marketing
- differentiated (or segmented) marketing
- undifferentiated (or mass) marketing.

**Positioning** involves the formulation of a definitive marketing strategy around which the product would be marketed to the target audience. Porter identified four positioning strategies:

- cost leadership
- differentiation
- cost focus
- differentiation focus.

## How the finance function interacts with sales and marketing

The modern approach is for the two functions to collaborate (assisted by technology), working as business partners and utilising each other's specialisms.

| | |
|---|---|
| **Budgeting** | Finance will discuss the likely sales volume with sales and marketing, in order to produce the sales budget. |
| **Advertising** | Finance will help in setting the budget and in monitoring the benefit generated. |
| **Pricing** | Finance will have an input into setting the optimum price. |
| **Market share** | Finance can provide sales volume information and help to determine market share. |
| **KPIs** | Finance will help to establish and monitor the KPIs for sales and marketing. |

**Two specific areas where this business partnering may enhance performance are:**

**Product/service development** – the finance function will work collaboratively with sales and marketing to evaluate new product/service lines.

**Product/service life-cycles and costing** – the finance function will interact with sales and marketing to consider the life-cycle costs and ensure a balanced portfolio.

- Unlocking the potential value of **big data** using real-time **data analytics** provides huge opportunities for the sales and marketing function.

- They will work with finance to gain this unique insight.

- Examples of big data analytics in marketing include:

| Highly specific **market segmentation and customisation** in real-time | Data used to enhance **product/ service development** | **Decision making** (such as pricing, inventory) enhanced through, say, realtime data visulalisation | **Obtaining customer feedback** to identify changes |

## Key performance indicators

| Example activity | Possible KPI |
| --- | --- |
| **Overall sales and marketing activity** | • Growth in sales volume/revenue<br>• Market share |
| **Promotion** | • Awareness levels<br>• Website traffic to conversion rate % |
| **Product/service** | • Product development time/cost<br>• Brand value |
| **Pricing** | • Price relative to industry average<br>• Price elasticity of demand |
| **Place** | • Transport costs<br>• Storage costs |

# how the finance function interacts with human resources

managing finance in a digital world

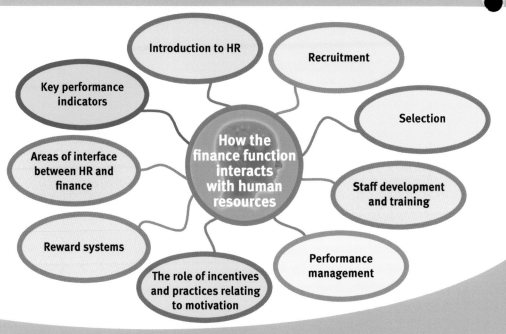

## Introduction to HR

The HR function is responsible for the management and development of human resources within the organisation. Their role includes the creation, development and maintenance of an effective workforce, matching the requirements of an organisation to the environment and responding to that environment.

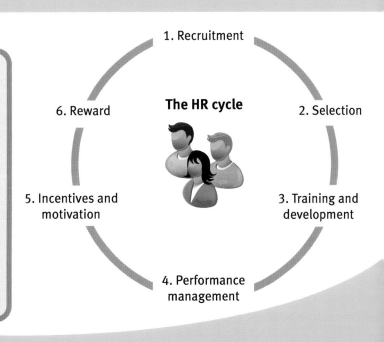

1. Recruitment

6. Reward

**The HR cycle**

2. Selection

5. Incentives and motivation

3. Training and development

4. Performance management

**Recruitment** involves attracting a pool of suitable candidates for the job.

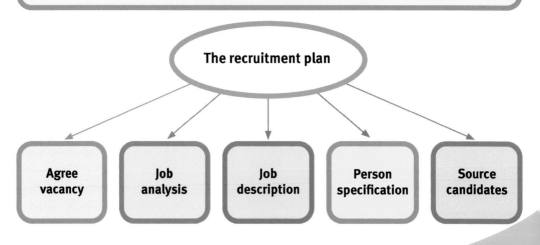

The recruitment plan

- Agree vacancy
- Job analysis
- Job description
- Person specification
- Source candidates

**Selection** is aimed at choosing the best person for the job from the field of candidates sourced via recruitment.

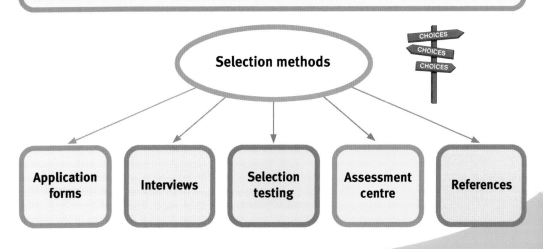

**Training** is the planned and systematic modification of behaviour through learning events, programmes and instruction which enable individuals to achieve the level of knowledge, skills and competence to carry out their work effectively.

**Development** is the growth or realisation of a person's ability and potential through conscious or unconscious learning and educational experiences.

## The training and development process:

1. Identify training and development needs
2. Set training objectives
3. Plan the training
4. Deliver the training
5. Evaluate the training

Step 5 includes four levels: reaction, learning, behaviour, results.

## Performance management

| 1. SMART targets set at the beginning of the period | 2. Monitor performance during the period | 3. Review performance in appraisal at the end of the period | 4. Action plan agreed with new targets for the next period |
|---|---|---|---|

Lockett's six **barriers to effective appraisal** are confrontation, judgement, chat, bureaucracy, annual event, unfinished business.

## Incentives and practices relating to motivation

- The psychological contract

- Employee involvement

- Workforce flexibility

A **reward system** refers to all the monetary, non-monetary and psychological payments that an organisation provides for its employees in exchange for the work they perform. Rewards can be divided into three categories:

- **Basic pay** – the minimum annual salary or hourly rate the employee receives.

- **Performance-related pay** – rewards such as bonuses or share options based on the achievement of individual, team or organisational SMART objectives.

- **Benefits** – a range of flexible rewards such as pensions, company cars and health insurance.

The **modern approach to HR is to view people as one of the greatest assets of the organisation** and that finance and HR should work together more closely (assisted by technology) with the 'people as assets' as their focus.

**Examples of areas of interface include:**

- Ensuring compliance with relevant laws and regulations

- Performance management and appraisal

- Considering the costs and benefits of different HR policies

## Key performance indicators

| Example activity | Possible KPI |
|---|---|
| **Recruitment and selection** | • Cost per employee hired<br>• Female to male ratio |
| **Training and development** | • Impact of training on existing KPIs<br>• Training feedback |
| **Performance management** | • Appraisals completed on time<br>• Appraisal action plan agreed and followed up |
| **Motivation** | • Turnover rate<br>• Employee satisfaction scores |
| **Reward systems** | • Competitiveness of reward system<br>• Adherence to laws and regulations |

# how the finance function interacts with IT

managing finance in a digital world

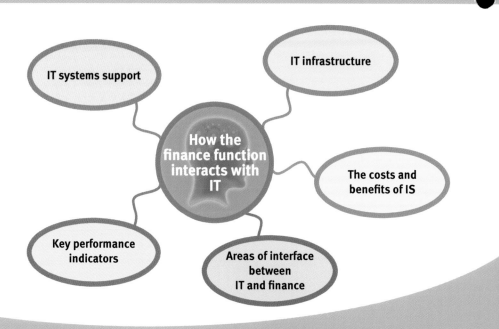

## IT systems support

**Information systems (IS)** refer to the provision and management of information to support the running of an organisation.

**Information technology (IT)** is the supporting equipment (hardware) that provides the infrastructure to run the information systems.

The **IT function** is responsible for planning, evaluating, installing, operating and maintaining the hardware, software, networks and data centres required by the organisation.

A **management information system (MIS)** converts internal and external data into useful information which is then communicated to managers at all levels and across all functions to enable them to make timely and effective decisions.

**Key types of MIS:**

| | |
|---|---|
| **Executive information system (EIS)** | • User friendly internal/external information for senior executives.<br>• Summarised form with an option to 'drill' down to the detail. |
| **Decision support system (DSS)** | • Predicts possible consequences of different scenarios.<br>• Managers then use judgement to make decisions. |
| **Transaction processing system (TPS)** | • Used by operational managers to make decisions.<br>• Records and summarises daily, routine transactions. |
| **Expert system** | • Hold specialist knowledge, for example on law, taxation.<br>• Non-experts from all levels of management can utilise. |

**Knowledge** is the application of a cognitive process to information so that it becomes useful. Knowledge can be **explicit** or **tacit.**

**Knowledge management systems** refer to any type of IT that helps to capture, store, retrieve and use knowledge to enhance the knowledge management process.

Examples include groupware, intranets, extranets, data warehouses, decision support systems and document management systems.

**IT infrastructure** consists of the core networks, databases, software, hardware and procedures managed by the IT function. A good IT infrastructure can enable organisational transformation in a number of ways:

- the adoption of new ways of working

- productivity improvements

- multi-source data capture and analysis

- the creation of shared service capability

- digitisation of information

- flexible working practices and virtual organisations (see below).

Two significant ways in which technology has enabled transformation is the increase in **remote working** (sometimes called **teleworking** or **homeworking**) and the formation of **virtual teams**.

### Advantages of remote working

- Lower infrastructure costs

- Increased employee motivation, productivity and commitment

- Helps attract and retain employees

- Lower absenteeism and staff turnover

### Disadvantages of remote working

- Co-ordination and control of staff difficult

- Employee motivation, productivity and commitment may actually reduce

- Dilution of organisational culture

- Some additional labour cost

**A virtual organisation** outsources most or all functions to other organisations and simply exists as a network of contracts, with very few, if any, functions being kept in-house.

**A virtual team** is a group of people who interact through independent tasks guided by a common purpose and work across space, time and organisational boundaries with links strengthened by IT.

## The costs and benefits of IS

The finance function can assist the IT function in carrying out a **cost-benefit analysis** to decide whether the potential benefits of a new IS justify the costs.

Some different costs and benefits of IS are covered on the next two pages.

## Privacy and security

IS have huge potential **benefits** to the organisation but come at a potential **cost** in terms of privacy and security threats and solutions.

| Threat | Solution |
|---|---|
| **Natural disasters** | Fire procedures |
| **Malfunction** | Back-up procedures |
| **Unauthorised access** | Access control |
| **Viruses** | Anti-virus software |
| **Hackers** | Firewall software, data encryption |
| **Human error** | Training |
| **HR risk** | Ergonomic design of workstation |

The **systems architecture** is the way the systems are organised together to support the organisation's function and goals. Systems can be **centralised or decentralised** and there will be **costs** and **benefits** associated with each of these.

**Data flow** is the movement of data through a process or system and includes data input, processing, output and storage. Good data flows will result in **benefits** but will have an associated **cost**.

**Big data information management** will unlock the potential value of big data but this **benefit** will come at a **cost** to the organisation.

## Areas of interface between IT and finance

**Traditionally,** the IT function and the finance function worked independently. Finance viewed IT as a cost whereas the IT function viewed it as an **asset**. Collaboration was limited, for example to establishing a budget for a new IT system.

The **modern** approach is to view IT as one of the **greatest assets** of the organisation and that finance and IT should work more closely resulting in, for example:

- smarter investment in IT

- improvements in information security and compliance

- improved data analytics

- cost-benefit analysis.

## Key performance indicators

| Example activity | Possible KPI |
| --- | --- |
| **Operational** activities – KPIs used to monitor the day to day activity and effectiveness of the IT function | • Ticket response rates for IT issues sent to IT support<br>• System/technology downtime |
| **Transformational** activities – KPIs used to measure impact of IT initiatives on decision making | • Cost of new technology<br>• Time saved using new technology |
| **Strategic** activities – KPIs used to monitor the progress of the IT function towards strategic goals | • Revenue generated using new technology<br>• Technology leading to competitive advantage |

The CIMA Official Revision Cards are the only printed revision aids endorsed by CIMA. They provide complete coverage of the CIMA syllabus in bite-sized chunks and will help cement your knowledge and understanding.

Based upon research into learning styles and effective recall they:

- are highly visual and colourful which will be particularly effective for visual learners
- can be rearranged and reorganized so they will appeal to kinaesthetic learners who prefer to learn by doing
- reduce the content to the most important areas, making it far easier to digest and identify the relationships between key topics
- include handy exam tips and guidance on topic weighting.

Their small size makes them ideal for use anywhere, at home in the classroom or on the move.

2022 edition

Relevant for the 2019 CIMA professional qualification syllabus assessments

ISBN 978-1-78740-997-2

9 781787 409972 >

**Kaplan Publishing UK**
Unit 2, The Business Centre,
Molly Millars Lane,
Wokingham, Berkshire RG41 2QZ

Tel: +44 (0) 118 989 0629
Fax: +44 (0) 118 979 7455

Email: publishing@kaplan.co.uk
www.kaplanpublishing.co.uk

FSC
www.fsc.org
MIX
From responsible sources
FSC® C057352

CIMA®